FANCY PIGEONS

Aad Rijs

FANCY PIGEONS

REBO
PUBLISHERS

© 2003 Zuid Boekprodukties
© 2006 Rebo Publishers

Text: Aad Rijs
Layout and cover design: AdAm Studio, Prague, The Czech Republic
Typesetting and pre-press services: A. R. Garamond, Prague,
The Czech Republic
Translation: Abandon Agency, Prague, The Czech Republic
Proofreading: Sarah Dunham

ISBN 13: 978-90-366-1442-9
ISBN 10: 90-366-1442-2

Contents

1   KEEPING PIGEONS

History

Since the dawn of human history pigeons have been kept as pets. Examples thereof are amply available in literature. One of the best known stories concerning pigeons is the story of the flood in the Old Testament. In this story Noah, who has a suspicion the waters are receding and land is surfacing again, releases a pair of doves. These returned carrying green olive branches in their beaks. In the beginning people kept pigeons because of their useful contribution to everyday life. The pigeon provided tasty meat and high quality manure and was popular as a sacrificial animal in religious ceremonies. Over the centuries interest grew not only in the useful qualities of domesticated pigeons, but also in deviating shapes and different ways of flying. Anomalies that were seen as interesting were consciously bred. This is how breeds with a distinctive flying style were created – Tumblers, Rollers, Highflyers, Endurance Flyers

An historic large dovecote meant for the production of meat and manure

and Homing Pigeons. The diversity in shapes however is even greater. For example, there are giant pigeons and miniature pigeons, slender breeds with beautiful colors and heavy breeds that were originally kept for their meat. One of the best known breeds with an aberrant shape that is only kept for pleasure is the Fantail which, because of a mutation, has an excessive amount of tail feathers. This creates the appealing raised and fan-shaped tail.

Type of enthusiast

The pigeon has by now lost its significance as a producer of manure for agriculture. Pigeon manure is still used, but on a relatively small scale. Keeping pigeons for their meat is still done commercially. The size of the industry worldwide is small, but as is common in this century, of an intensive nature. What hasn't diminished over time but has, on the contrary, seen massive growth is the interest in keeping pigeons as a hobby.

There are three categories of enthusiasts :
- Those who like to fly pigeons (Homing Pigeons and flying style enthusiasts)
- Those who like to keep and breed wild pigeon species
- Those who like to keep and/or breed Fancy Pigeons

What all these people have in common is the pleasure they derive from taking care of pigeons. It really doesn't matter that much whether you keep pigeons that have to achieve a goal or pigeons which are bred purely for their looks, as long as you enjoy taking care of and observing the pigeons.

The Fantail might be the most well known domesticated pigeon

Don't buy on impulse, but make a well thought-out decision

> **Domesticated**
> Domesticated pigeons are birds that, depending on species, can become moderately to very tame and that may be very strongly oriented towards their caretaker. Because of their social character it is best to house them in groups.

Things to consider

If you consider keeping pigeons you have to decide several things for yourself. Making these considerations costs a lot of time and energy, but is a lot better than impulsively buying pigeons just because you thought they were pretty. If the pigeon breed, owner and circumstances are not well adjusted to each other, then the initial enthusiasm with which you started often turns into a disappointment which results in the pigeons having to leave. The things you should consider are:

How to house the birds

How many pigeons can you or do you want to keep and how do you want to house them? This is one of the first things you should ask yourself. If you just want to keep two or three pairs of pigeons then there is always enough space on a dovecote. However, this does mean the birds will always fly out in the open. This may be problematic depending on the circumstances and the tolerance of your neighbors. Keeping larger amounts of pigeons requires larger accommodation. This requires both space and money, but you also have to consider what you may or may not build. It

An aviary also offers the opportunity for necessary exercise

might very well be that you need to apply for a building permit or that you have an obligation to report building activities. Also you need to consider whether or not you want to occasionally give the pigeons the opportunity to fly out in the open or if you only want to give them the opportunity to fly in an aviary. This is in part connected to the breed that you are planning to keep. The desire to fly, the instinct to find the way back home, the flight velocity and the height at which the bird flies is very dependent on breed. This makes some breeds easy prey for predatory birds and cats and other breeds not at all. If there is a lot of disruption from wild cats and/or predatory birds then this should certainly be considered.

To breed or not to breed
Another thing you need to ask yourself when deciding to keep pigeons is whether or not you want to breed them. Responsible breeding requires a different kind of accommodation (multiple pigeon lofts) and a different setup than you would need if you just accommodated a couple of pigeons with whom you don't intend to breed. However, this last possibility is not easy because pigeons have such a strong instinct for procreation that they will build a nest, lay eggs and raise young even under the worst of circumstances. The multitude of neglected pigeons in cities is evident proof of that.

Providing care

Regardless of the breed or the purpose, pigeons require, just like any other pet, regular and quality care and appropriate accommodation. Keeping pigeons in a responsible way means that you have the obligation to provide daily care, which besides feeding and watering consists of cleaning the pigeon loft. This last thing can be a lot or a little work depending on the number of pigeons you intend to keep and the way the pigeon loft is set up. Among other things the implementation of grates as floors can prevent a lot of cleaning work, but it is a more expensive setup and requires a decision before you start building the pigeon loft.

The Saint is a pigeon which requires extra care

2 ACCOMMODATION

The basics

There are many different possibilities for accommodation. A simple wall-mounted nest box, a beautiful dovecote or a large pigeon loft with many separate compartments may all suffice as long as you take into account a number of basic rules.

To keep pigeons in good shape the housing has to be clean and well ventilated. Furthermore, pigeons only feel really good when they have housing that has a pleasant temperature. It is therefore ideal if the morning sun can shine into the housing. This means that the front of the loft needs to be situated on the southeastern side. However, this isn't always possible, especially if you are building a larger structure.

A decorative but not very practical dovecote

A well thought
out practical
dovecote

This dovecote is
easy to reach and
is also easy to
clean

Dovecote

Many dovecotes seem to be made as garden decoration rather than for the purpose of keeping pigeons. Pigeon holes are located on all sides and cleaning the inside is barely possible. It is therefore important that you take a good look at the design when you buy a dovecote. It is self-evident that the dovecote needs to be easily accessible and also easy to clean. Side panels which can be removed are an absolute necessity, as well as a solid firmly mounted pole which supports the whole construction. A smooth metal pole is ideal because it is impossible for cats to climb. Pigeon holes all around it are pointless because those openings, after mounting the dovecote to face north, will only allow cold and moisture to be blown inside. The dovecote has to be divided into sections with a pigeon hole for every section – this brings peace and prevents draft. The number of couples that are lofted on a dovecote should always be less than the number of available sections because pigeons, you see, enjoy picking their own section. There also always has to be a possibility for the young pigeons to claim their own spot on the dovecote. If you don't allow for this the young pigeons will leave the dovecote to wander about as soon as they are able to fly. Their parents are already working on the next brood and don't accept the young pigeons' presence in their section

anymore. If you are unable to find a ready-made dovecote that takes these specifications into account then you should consider making a dovecote following your own design or have one made.

A separate feeding area has many advantages

Practical matters in and around the dovecote

Pigeons that live on a dovecote also need to be fed and watered daily. One option is that you scatter a handful of feed on the ground in the vicinity of the dovecote every day. However, this is not ideal. First of all, the immediate vicinity is often dirtied by droppings and secondly, pigeons are easy prey for cats when on the ground. It is better to place an open cabinet close to the dovecote with food and drink bowls inside. The pigeons get used to this pretty quickly and can eat in peace in a responsible way. In fact, if you set out the food at regular times each day you will find that they sit and wait for it. Another good solution is to design part of the dovecote as a feeding area.

When new pigeons arrive on the dovecote they will at first have to get used to their new accommodation. Therefore you need a (temporary) chicken wire front around the dovecote. After a week the newcomers will have bonded enough with their new accommodation, especially if there is nesting space available and they know the area enough so that they can now be set free.

A wall-mounted nesting box

In general, the same guidelines which apply to a dovecote also apply to a wall-mounted nesting box. Naturally, when you position it you have less choice as regards the direction of the wind. If the box is placed in a very unfavorable spot then make sure that the pigeon holes are generously shielded from above so as to ward off rain and wind. Also take into account uninvited guests such as cats. Here the box should not only be out of reach from the ground, but also from above. If the box is too close to the edge of the roof

*A practical garden
loft with an aviary
attached*

A good ceiling construction ensures optimal ventilation

then cats have the opportunity to jump onto the top of the box from the roof.

A pigeon loft

If you decide to place a freestanding pigeon loft in your garden then you have the possibility of either buying an existing pigeon loft or building one yourself. The last option gives you more possibilities as regards dimensions, but the disadvantage for the inexperienced enthusiast is that you are likely to make mistakes in the design. Of course, buying a pigeon loft from a manufacturer is more expensive, but a lot of experience from other enthusiasts has been taken into account in the design. For a pigeon loft in the garden, insulated wood construction with a tiled roof and a floor about twenty centimeters from the ground is the most suitable. The height of the floor ensures that no moisture can creep up into the loft and also has the advantage that the wind blowing under the loft keeps the bottom dry. However, to prevent too much wind and cold under the loft, make sure the sides and the back go all the way to the ground. A roof made from tiles without roof sheathing ensures good air circulation within the pigeon loft. To protect the pigeons from draft, a ceiling is placed under the roof. This ceiling completely covers the perches of the pigeons, but doesn't go from wall to wall. At the front of the loft the ceiling has to be open in order to allow air to flow to the tiled roof. Make sure the opening is closed off with chicken wire or grates so that the pigeons can't get onto the ceiling. It would be ideal if you could adjust the opening which enables you to adjust the amount of airflow.

The pigeon loft: dimensions

To place a pigeon loft you will have to, depending on the zoning laws in your community, report it or obtain a building permit. In either case you will have to have a building plan. If you buy a prefabricated pigeon loft from a manufacturer then they will usually be willing to assist you with the necessary paperwork. You usually have a duty to report up to 50 cubic meters in volume. These dimensions are usually sufficient for most enthusiasts. You can then build a pigeon loft that is about 7 x 3 meters. As a rule of thumb, for the number of pigeons you can loft you can place at most one couple per cubic meter – but this is only a rule of thumb. The actual space required is very much dependent on the size of the pigeons, the character of the breed (restless or not) and whether or not they are free flying. Don't count on using less than one cubic meter per couple. A pigeon loft of 7 x 3 meters with an average height of 2.20 meters has a volume of 46.20 cubic meters and therefore only offers enough space for at most 45 couples or 90 pigeons.

A small loft can suffice as long as the pigeons are able to fly free

Setting up a loft: several sections

If you decide to breed the pigeons in a pigeon loft to which you as caretaker have access yourself, then you need to

divide the loft into at least two sections. You have to take care of this as soon as you build. You need this partition in order to let your young pigeons, as soon as they can eat and drink independently, grow up separately from the older pigeons. In the part of the pigeon loft where they were born, the young pigeons are too harassed by the older pigeons which see the independent young as intruders into their territory.

Depending on the nature of the pigeon breed this can lead to violent hunting and pecking at the young animals – sometimes until they bleed. A separate section for the young animals guarantees rest while they grow up. At the end of the breeding season (at the latest end of June or the beginning of July) a "young pigeon section" can also be used to loft the grown hens with their young. The grown cocks stay in the section in which the breeding took place. The young pigeons from the first and second round of breeding which are clearly recognizable as cocks can then be moved from the "young pigeon section" to the section with the grown cocks. Through this separation of the sexes, the laying of eggs comes to an end and the animals enter a phase of rest in which they start to moult. If the animals would stay sexually active for too long, then moulting would start too late and their plumage would not be ready in time. This would mean lessened resistance against the bad weather in fall. Even better is of course to separate even more sections in the pigeon loft, so that young animals don't

A pigeon loft with several sections and spacious flights

A white wall gets dirty quickly and starts to look sloppy

have to mix with older ones. This means a lower possibility of the transmission of viruses from the hardened adult animals to the sensitive younger animals.

Are you my downstairs neighbor?

How to treat the walls on the inside

The walls on the inside of the pigeon loft can be treated with latex or with similar (non-toxic) products, but you can also leave the walls untreated. It is better not to use bright colors. Not treating the wood or the use of soothing colors ensures the light is not too bright. The pigeon is a rock dweller by nature and feels safer against a dark background rather than a lighter one. What you use to treat the walls is not that important as long as the wall is able to breathe. Sealing the wall with paint or varnish is absolutely wrong because this prevents intake of moisture by the walls. This makes the climate in the pigeon loft damp which is bad for the pigeons.

Practical box perch which prevents fights for space

Don't put the perches on top of each other – you want to prevent soiling of the downstairs neighbor

Perches

In the part of the pigeon loft that is designated for young pigeons there have to be enough perches. The minimal number is one perch per pigeon. It is however better to create more perches than pigeons, in order to minimize fighting. The perch can consist of a so-called "V-perch" that is connected to the wall or of a cupboard that has a nesting box for every pigeon. Place the perches in such a way that the higher placed pigeons can't dirty their lower placed colleagues with their droppings. Both the V-perches and the so-called box perches provide this. Besides the perches it is advisable to equip the pigeon loft with a windowsill. The pigeons enjoy using this to lie in the sun or to parade up and down. The young cocks that are becoming aware of their manhood will frequently fly from their perches to the board and twirl around their mates while dragging their tails.

Perches for muffed pigeons

For pigeons which have a large muff of feathers around their feet, box perches and V-perches are less suitable because the feathers come into contact with the walls; this results in broken feathers. For these breeds round perches on a carrier are usually used. The carrier ensures sufficient distance from the wall. These perches can't be mounted on top of each other, because the lower placed pigeons will be soiled with the droppings of the more highly perched loft mate.

Feed container and water container

The windowsill with parading cocks

Place the feed container on the floor of the pigeon loft. This has to be long enough to enable all the pigeons present in the loft to eat at the same time. This feed container needs a construction that prevents pigeons from getting into the

container because this causes contamination of the feed. The top of the container needs to be provided with a closed lid or an easily spinning roll for the same reason. This last system doesn't provide the pigeons with enough grip, thereby making sure that they don't sit on the container. These containers can be bought ready-made at exhibitions and stores for agricultural needs but they have one disadvantage: they are designed for average-size pigeons. For the smallest breeds of Fancy Pigeons the spokes are too far apart which does enable the pigeons to contaminate the food by sitting in it. The solution is to either modify the ready-made food container or to make one (or have one made) to size. Of course, the pigeon loft also needs a water container. The water must always be clean. This isn't easy in a pigeon loft because there is always dust and down feathers in the air. For this reason it is best to provide the water container with a closed lid and to make the openings through which the pigeons drink as small as possible. The ready-made drinking containers which are on the market

Pigeons with feathered feet like this Trumpeter require special perches

do a good job of this. A simple method of preventing pollution of the pigeon loft with down feathers is by placing a loose board at a slant against the back wall. The down feathers will accumulate behind it as a result of the air currents that are caused by the flying of the pigeons. This is a simple but effective solution that, especially during the moulting season, prevents a lot of pollution.

The floor of the pigeon loft

The floor of the pigeon loft can be covered with sand, straw, woodchips or a grate. Uncovered floors are also sometimes found. This last option means that you have to scrape manure twice a day in order to guarantee a clean loft. If you don't have much time, grates or some kind of covering for the floor is a better solution. Dry sand that is sifted at least twice a week (for droppings and feathers) makes for a *You can buy lots* pigeon loft that looks well cared for and in which the *of useful* manure stays dry. Straw and woodchips often stay quite a *accessories at fairs* long time in the pigeon loft. The manure stays dry but the

number of feathers the pigeons lose accumulates and this looks very untidy. Grated floors have the advantage that the manure falls through them as well as feathers, especially most of the downy ones. This keeps the pigeon loft looking tidy all the time.

Using grated floors means that the pigeon loft needs to be well ventilated and extremely dry. Dried up manure under the grates is no problem, but wet manure is a source of bacterial infections. The solution to choose depends on the amount of time you have available and the options the pigeon loft offers you. Regardless of how you cover the floor, the necessity remains to regularly remove the manure from the perches and the "catwalk" in front of the window. It is best to do this every day. Make a habit of doing this while you feed the birds; the amount of work is relatively small and it prevents contamination of the pigeons and possible infections.

Woodchips create a lot of dust and are not suitable material for covering the floor

Beech cuttings form an excellent floor covering

Nest boxes

Despite plenty of perches for the pigeons, there has to be plenty of space for hatching eggs in the breeding section of the pigeon loft. Pigeons want to have their own space where the couple is lord and master, which ensures peace and quiet during the hatching of the eggs and the raising of the young. This means that there has to be at least one nest box available for every pigeon couple. Being in excess is better however, because pigeons are very particular and sometimes there are fierce battles for the best spots. Once all couples have found a spot for themselves you close the extra nest boxes in order to restore peace to the pigeon loft.

Very well thought out nest boxes can be bought ready-made, but they are easy to make for anyone with some affinity with tools. The size of the boxes should be adapted to the size of the pigeons; it's better that they are too big than too small. The minimum size for a nest box is 60 centimeters wide, 50 centimeters deep and fifty centimeters high. The nesting boxes need to be provided with a front that can be closed. This enables you to lock up the pigeons during breeding, and prevents the nest boxes from being used year round. Nest boxes are usually placed in rows in several layers on top of each other at the back of the pigeon loft. Make sure you fully utilize the available space and that no space is left open. If there is any room left between the upper nest boxes and the roof of the pigeon loft then the pigeons will always try to get into this space in order to breed there. It will, at the very least be a place where dirt accumulates and which is difficult to clean. It is customary to not treat the fronts of the nest boxes or to paint them white. This looks very neat but can be confusing for the pigeons. After all, all the nest boxes look alike which can result in pigeons accidentally flying into the wrong nest boxes, causing fights and disorder. Pigeons are quite capable of distinguishing

A practical nest box for small breeds

bright colors. By painting the front of each nesting box in a different color the pigeons are able to find their own territory without fail. After the breeding season the nest boxes are locked up and only the cocks remain in this section of the pigeon loft. It is the start of the moulting season and peace and quiet in the pigeon loft is important. By removing the nest boxes and replacing them with perches, the "territorial instincts" connected with the nest boxes are removed. If the nest boxes can't be removed then placing a

detachable wall in front of the nest boxes is a good alternative. The wall can be used in turn to place more perches.

Nest boxes: a half open front.

Often the front is constructed from two parts which can
turn. Once the pigeons are used to their own nest box and
the hatching has started then one part is opened. This sim-
plifies flying into the nest box. It also helps strange pigeons
who are not one of the couple to quickly escape from the
wrong nest box if they accidentally fly into it, preventing
violent fights. However, a disadvantage to this half-open
front is that young pigeons, who after two weeks already
saunter a little outside the nest, sometimes leave the nest
box too soon. These young pigeons that have fallen out of
the nest box are sometimes strongly harassed by the other
pigeons. This problem can be prevented by applying a small
steel bar door which you can open that provides good access
to the nest box and a solid front that has a flap that enables
the pigeons to fly in. The opening of this flap should be
about 12.5 centimeters from the bottom of the nest box.
The young pigeons won't be able to surmount this height
until they are really ready to fly out.

It is possible to breed on the floor, but the young leave home too early

Ventilation in the pigeon loft: a must

For pigeon lofts of all sizes it is true that good ventilation is a necessity to guarantee the health of the animals. A pigeon loft which is cleaned regularly, well ventilated, and doesn't contain too many pigeons smells clean. For the pigeons this is important because they use a lot of oxygen. For you this is important because otherwise, as the daily caretaker, you would breathe too much so-called "pigeon dust." This pigeon dust consists mainly of proteins which pigeons excrete when they defecate. These specific proteins can cause an allergic reaction in humans. One of the most common signs of that is shortness of breath and tightness of the chest. This reaction is referred to as a "pigeon's lung." It depends on your personal sensitivity, the time you spend in the pigeon loft and how well the pigeon loft is ventilated whether or not you will have to deal with this problem. You can reduce the chances of developing this allergy in a number of ways:

- Wear a dust mask in the pigeon loft that covers nose and mouth
- Don't expose too much skin to the dust in the pigeon loft by wearing a dust-coat when you are with the pigeons

- Be careful while you are cleaning to not get too much dust flying in the air
- Make sure the pigeons are outside the pigeon loft when you are cleaning. Pigeons flying around while you are cleaning tend to send a lot of dust flying

You can also try to prevent a possible pigeon lung by the way you set up the pigeon loft. When you choose to cover the floor with sand, straw or woodchips then this means that you leave a lot of manure at the bottom of the pigeon loft and that there are therefore many protein particles in the pigeon loft. A better solution is not to cover the floor at all and to remove the manure every day. However, this does involve a lot of work. A good alternative is applying manure grates above the floor of the pigeon loft. If the pigeon loft is sufficiently dry, this accumulation of manure under the grate won't create any problems for the climate in the pigeon loft and also no extra dust.

Open-fronted pigeon loft: ideal ventilation

For Fancy Pigeons that don't fly around a lot but are kept in aviaries, an open-fronted pigeon loft is an excellent alternative. This is an aviary that is closed on all sides with the exception of the (broad) front which consists entirely of chicken wire. As long as pigeons are able to sit dry and out of the wind this setup will keep them in excellent condition. The advantage for the caretaker is that the pigeon dust is hardly any trouble and the pigeon loft is always airy.

This system can be copied in a pigeon loft with a closed front by completely opening the windows and equipping the windows with a chicken wire front. If the front of the pigeon loft isn't pointing southeast but is pointed in a less favorable direction and you're afraid rain might get in, then covering the front part of the aviary with transparent corrugated plastic sheets or mounting a transparent canopy is a solution.

Exercise: the flight

To give the animals which do not have the opportunity to fly about freely enough exercise, a flight or aviary is added to the pigeon loft. Sun, wind and rain ensure that the animals get good naturally-built resistance. If you've got the space, make the flight as large as possible. In this aspect length is more important than width. After all, you want to give the pigeons the opportunity to fly. If you only have a little or even no space, then a chicken wire enlargement of the front can be a partial solution. Even though it doesn't provide any extra flying space it does allow the animals to enjoy the air outside.

The flight should preferably be made from finely meshed chicken wire so that sparrows and other birds are kept outside. This prevents lice and viral infections through direct contact of the pigeons with wild birds. The flight has to be accessible for the caretaker because strict demands for hygiene apply. Because of this, the best thing to put on the floor of the flight is river sand. This is easy to clean. Even better is a floor made of grates about twenty centimeters above the floor with a concrete or tiled floor underneath. This prevents the pigeons from coming in contact with their own manure at the bottom of the flight. This means that the pigeons are cleaner and healthier; worm infections especially are prevented by these precautions.

Little space, but still fresh air!

The grates have of course to be removable so that the manure under the grated floor can be regularly removed. You mount a number of perches in the flight; a rectangular slat, of which the edges have been rounded with the help of a planer and some sandpaper, is perfect for this task. Don't mount more than two but do place them as far apart as possible. This forces the pigeons to use their wings and after all, that is the point. You can cover the top of the flight with just chicken wire but you can also completely or partially cover it with transparent corrugated plastic sheets. This last part depends on how the flight is situated in regard to the prevailing wind. If there is no chance of rain getting into the pigeon loft, then a chicken wire roof on the flight is preferable.

Loft with a spacious flight and a practical grated floor

Choosing free flying or not?

Many Fancy Pigeon enthusiasts don't let their pigeons fly free anymore. There are various reasons for this; possible nuisance for neighbors is one of them. A reason that is a lot more common is the badly developed flying instinct of

Free flying animals can easily be lost

many Fancy Pigeon breeds. The animals do fly, but only very short distances and they often can't find their way back to their own pigeon loft. Also, predatory birds take their toll. A rather slow Fancy Pigeon is often easy prey. This means that free flying can cost you a lot of animals. These are often valuable breeding animals. This inability to fly well and loss of the orientation instinct may sound strange

Cats, but also some dogs do sometimes have an eye out for pigeons

if you realize that Fancy Pigeons were originally kept free flying. By breeding on bodily characteristics there was sometimes (too) little consideration for flying abilities. Many breeds of Tumblers for example will barely tumble when allowed to fly free. Only a few enthusiasts pay specific attention to flying capabilities and don't care that the pigeons in the pigeon loft are not quite as beautiful provided they paint a beautiful picture in the sky.

Threats from the sky

If you allow your pigeons to enjoy free flight then you should be very aware of the fact that sooner or later fewer pigeons will return than you set free. Threats like cats, traffic, electricity cables, weather conditions and predatory birds are circumstances which cause every enthusiast to lose a number of his animals every year. The best thing therefore is to let the pigeons get used to the surroundings, to flying free and to their own pigeon house from a very young age when they are still barely able to

A fun race to have free flying, the Portuguese Tumbler

fly. It is best to do this when the weather is beautiful and clear. By placing them on the landing board or a so-called "sputnik," they have the opportunity to get to know the surroundings of the pigeon loft. During the following days you allow the young pigeons the opportunity to fly onto the roof of the pigeon loft. Soon the young animals will become more adventurous and start to undertake short flights around the loft. A good way to ensure the animals will return to the pigeon loft is by releasing them when they are hungry and to only feed them when they re-enter the loft. Also, for fully grown animals this is a good method which prevents the pigeons from roving around the

A Buzzard doesn't pose a threat to your pigeons

This Eastern Roller makes a preliminary survey of the surrounding of the loft from a sputnik

Good individual perches create peace outside the breeding season

neighborhood. The idea behind letting them fly free is after all to give the pigeons some exercise and to prevent them from just lazing around the pigeon loft. The latter only increases the chance that your animals will become a bother to the neighbors because the pigeons perch on the surrounding roofs and it makes them easy prey for cats and predatory birds.

Predatory birds

Predatory birds don't limit themselves to swooping down on a wild pigeon or dove; Fancy Pigeons are a beloved and often easy prey. Because their color and flying habits differ from those of wild pigeons, Fancy Pigeons are often easier to catch. Not all predatory birds constitute a threat, however. A number of them only hunt prey that lives on the ground. Pigeons are usually on to this and therefore don't panic when, for example, a Kestrel is flying by. However, if a Peregrine Falcon is in the neighborhood then you have to look out. One of the common predatory birds which love pigeons is the Sparrowhawk. Once one of these rogues has

an eye on your birds then he will start a fanatic pursuit, sometimes even all the way into the loft. Also Northern Goshawks, which nowadays can be found in reasonable numbers in the more wooded parts of Europe form a threat to your pigeons. Predatory birds like the Buzzard usually don't hunt pigeons and certainly not flying pigeons.

The Peregrine Falcon has an eye out for your pigeons

3 PURCHASE

What do you want?

The best rule of thumb when it comes to purchasing animals is never to buy animals spontaneously just because they look cute. If you haven't thought about it thoroughly and aren't well prepared, then getting a pet is irresponsible. The proof can be found in various pounds and pet shelters. With larger animals like dogs and cats there is at least a financial threshold to the purchase of pets. With pigeons that threshold is considerably lower, which makes the danger of impulsive decisions bigger. Before you buy you should have the housing sorted and have it ready for the breed you want to keep. For example, you need to know if you want to keep a small or a large breed and whether or not you want to breed them. Of course, you will have considered whether or not to keep the animals free flying or if they need to be content with a pigeon loft and an aviary.

Chimneysweeps:
the breed for you?

Which breed?

Besides all of the above, it is wise to choose the breed you want to purchase with care. If you are drawn to the beautiful color patterns of a Color Pigeon then you need to consider that these are usually rather shy pigeons with which you, as an enthusiast, will have trouble bonding. It is a shame if you don't discover this until after you purchase them. A disappointment of this nature usually means the pigeons go back to the dealer and that the search for pigeons begins anew. The characters of the pigeon and the owner have to be suited to each other. If you want uncomplicated breeding to which you don't have to pay too much attention then you shouldn't succumb to the charm of, for example the King Pigeon or the Gaditano Pouter Pigeon. Both species have their own specific breeding problems which can lead to a lot of disappointment if you aren't prepared for it. Long before purchase you should acquaint yourself with the different breeds and their attributes. Make a choice based on rational considerations and then try to find a place where you can purchase the breed of your choice. The time you spend preparing your choice will be amply compensated by the pleasure you will experience from choosing a breed that suits you.

A healthy pigeon
like this Hyacinth
Pigeon keeps a
sharp eye out and
is fully feathered

Purchase

You can make an attempt at the various dealers and have a look round at small animal fairs. The problem with this is that usually they just don't have what you are looking for available and many people are subsequently tempted to then just buy something which is available. Buying from dealers and at fairs has another disadvantage: many animals are put together in one space. This increases the chance that animals which have a disease will infect other animals. Not all enthusiasts are equally conscientious, so pigeons who haven't been vaccinated and pigeons that are sick do end up with dealers. Dealers are aware of this risk and will do all they can to avoid purchasing sick animals. The risk can however never be excluded.

Health

The present legislation concerning the trade in animals provides for a health guarantee but this doesn't extend past the purchase of the animals. If you place newly purchased animals with the pigeons you already own and these get sick as well then you have a problem that is not covered by any legal guarantee. Of course, this doesn't mean that you always get sick animals from a dealer; the opposite is rather true. Even when you buy from an enthusiast you run the risk of buying a sick animal. Therefore it is important to keep your eyes peeled. Typical for a healthy pigeon is that it's active, well feathered and produces dry manure. A pigeon whose feathers bulge and sits apathetically in its resting place and in addition produces thin, wet excrement you should never take home. In a cage, all of this is a little bit more difficult to judge; especially if you're not experienced. In a (large) pigeon loft a pigeon behaves more naturally and the deviant behavior will be more apparent. Therefore you should preferably buy the pigeons straight from the breeders' home. Here you have the greatest chance of getting both healthy animals and good advice.

Addresses

You can find the addresses of breeders by going through the classifieds in newspapers, on the internet or by approaching associations of breeders. You will also find some addresses at the back of this edition. Many breeds have an association that specializes in that breed. Sometimes this is a national association that focuses on only one breed, like for example

Many enthusiasts have more than one breed in their loft

the "Oudhollandse meeuwen" club. Although associations that focus on certain breed categories also exist. You can enquire about the addresses of various breed associations at the Fancy Pigeon Enthusiast national associations.

Season

The opportunity to buy pigeons strongly depends on the season. In the spring most enthusiasts don't have any animals available because they only have those animals left that they want to use for breeding. Part of the pigeon loft is empty and is being prepared for the arrival of the young pigeons. Almost nobody will at this point be willing to sell their carefully selected breeding animals to a new enthusiast. A much more suitable time to look for new pigeons is the fall or the early winter months. Almost every Fancy Pigeon breeder has at that time a surplus of young pigeons. This "surplus" consists of young healthy animals that often have a minor flaw. This makes the pigeons not comply with the ideal the enthusiast envisions. This ideal can be connected to either the appearance or the flying style. These

In the middle of the breeding season it is hard to purchase more pigeons

young pigeons however can be very useful as future breeding material. They are in any case suited to the enthusiast who is just looking for healthy pigeons in order to start his new hobby.

At the breeders'

Once you have found an address or a couple of addresses where you can buy the pigeons of your choice then you should make sure to head out well prepared. The housing is of course taken care of and food has been stocked. The number of pigeons you want to purchase is well thought out and the means of transport for your pigeons has been arranged. This last item is often forgotten, which makes people, as a last resort, opt for an empty box. Especially if it is hot you run the risk of not having enough fresh air getting into the box. All of this makes the purchase of a pigeon transport basket very sensible indeed. Once you've met the person you're buying from, you should take a good look around. Does the pigeon loft look well cared for and clean? Are the pigeons lively and are they well feathered? If so, then health probably won't be a problem. Always remember to enquire from the seller if the pigeons have been vaccinated against infectious diseases like paramyxo. You should also use your visit to the breeder to gain some specific knowledge about how to care for the breed. For example, pigeons with large and fully feathered feet ask for a little bit of extra attention in daily care and in breeding. If you plan to let the new animals fly free, then you should ask the breeder if the pigeons are used to free flight. If they aren't used to it, then be careful about letting them fly free. There is a substantial chance that you will lose a number of animals.

When you buy a German Double-Crested Trumpeter the salesman will provide you with a lot of information

Cock or Hen?

If you are being offered young animals it is always wise to
buy more than one couple. With pigeons the difference
between males (cocks) and females (hens) is difficult to see.
Sometimes the cocks are a little bit rougher around the
edges and a little heavier. The head also offers some clues
when trying to determine the gender. This however does
depend on breed. The real difference can only be determined through their behavior. A cock only shows that he is
a male when he becomes an adult. The time when this
occurs also depends on the breed. In reality, even the most
seasoned pigeon breeder makes a number of mistakes when
it comes to determining the gender of young pigeons. If you
have had to travel a great distance in order to get the dearly
coveted young pigeon couple and you discover at home that
you bought two cocks or two hens then this is quite a shame.
By buying more than one couple you are almost assured that
you at least bought one cock and one hen.

4   FOOD AND DRINK

Basic food

Pigeons belong to the species of seed eaters and therefore need to be provided with a diet that almost exclusively consists of grains, legumes and seeds. In the "pigeon world" there is a large variety of available mixtures of grains and seeds. Most of these have been developed by pigeon flying enthusiasts. Flying with pigeons can easily be compared with developments in professional sports. Depending on which achievement needs to be attained, for example a short or long distance flight, food is provided that is attuned to this achievement. Carbohydrates and proteins in the food are considered important indicators by these enthusiasts. For lovers of Fancy Pigeons however, other standards apply and the composition of the food hasn't yet been lifted into the realm of science. After all, these pigeons don't need to accomplish great achievements and they only require food that contains enough elements to keep their bodies in perfect condition during the winter period, during breeding and in the moulting season.

Pigeon food consists mainly of grains, seeds and legumes

Different kinds of food

The food manufacturers have composed a number of food mixtures that perform excellently. Within the species of Fancy Pigeons the food manufacturers distinguish heavy and light breeds, crop and non-crop breeds, breeds with red or light-red edged eyes and breeds with short or normal beaks. The length of the beak is the measure for the maximum size of the food to be eaten. In the so-called "short beak feed" for example, more coarse grain and legumes are absent. The food manufacturer selects based on these criteria, but at the same time makes sure to include smaller grains and legumes in the food so that the ideal mix of proteins and carbohydrates is achieved anyway. Always consult the brochure or the website of the food manufacturer of your choice and let the advice they give be your guide. Don't try to mix food yourself; without proper training and years of experience it is nearly impossible to determine a proper mix independently.

The occasional candy seed makes for tame pigeons

Here they are clearly feeding too much – besides, the food is polluted

---

Candy feed?

Besides the regular food it is not a problem to give the pigeons a little candy seed with the intent of making them better acquainted to you and to tame them. Nothing is more fun than when the pigeons come to sit down on the shoulder or the hand of their owner after being fed some fine seed.

How much food

There is quite a high percentage of barley in all pigeon feed and it is certain that pigeons don't like to eat this. The barley always remains in the feeding container till the end and is only eaten when the pigeons get hungry again. If half an hour after feeding there still is plenty of barley in the feeding container, then that means you fed them too much. The barley is therefore the ideal measuring stick for determining the amount of food your pigeons need; if everything is gone quickly then you are on the conservative side. If a lot of barley remains in the feeding container then you are

In case of free flight the pigeons themselves look for stones in the field

overfeeding. Barley you can add almost without repercussions. If the pigeons are a little bit fat at the end of winter just before the breeding season is about to start, then you can easily mix twenty to twenty five percent barley in the food mix. Barley consists mainly of carbohydrates and rough fiber. This means it fills well but contains few nutrients. This same remedy can be applied when the hens continue to lay eggs after the breeding season. That sometimes happens during warm, mild fall weather, even after they have been separated from the cocks.

A suitable container for providing grit, stomach stones or minerals

The red throat of this Old Dutch Capuchin betrays its visit to the mineral container

Grit and digestive stones

Grain and seed eaters to which pigeons also belong make use of little stones in their gizzards to grind to pieces the food that has been presoaked in their crop. Small stones are ground together like little millstones in their gizzards which crushes the grain and allows the nutrients to be absorbed into the digestive tract more easily. This supply of little stones is regularly replenished by the pigeon. If the pigeons are being allowed to fly free they will make sure of this themselves by landing in fields. Pigeons that don't have the opportunity to fly free of course don't have this opportunity. They therefore need to have a supply of little stones

A Danish Tumbler

available. A small bowl of stomach grit therefore needs to be present in the pigeon loft at all times. This is especially important for young pigeons and hens who are laying eggs. The pigeons only ingest it when they need it. Do make sure the stomach grit is regularly replenished because otherwise too much dust and dirt ends up in the bowl. Therefore it is much better to replenish a small bowl often than to let a large container stand around in the pigeon loft for months on end.

Vitamins, minerals and spore elements
The food which we give to our Fancy Pigeons consists largely of dried elements. Fresh grains and seeds are not recommended. Unripe seeds and grains are even dangerous as they can totally deregulate the bowels. To make sure the pigeons still get enough vitamins, minerals and spore elements there are various mixtures of additives for sale. You need to make these available to your pigeons at least once a week in a separate container. You will be surprised at the eagerness with which they absorb these mixtures; a clear sign that it is necessary. Some food manufacturers supply food to which vitamins, minerals and spore elements have been added in compressed form. This has the advantage that the pigeons get their requirements every day, stay in excellent condition and your job of feeding becomes easier.

Greens
Pigeons are not big on eating plants. Yet there are moments they like to eat greens, for example in spring. If the pigeons fly loose, then in this time of year we will see that the animals regularly pick at the young parts of the sprouting bottom dwellers. Pigeons which are kept indoors you can greatly please by giving them some finely chopped greens during the breeding season. Grated carrots are also a favorite. Weeds, such as chickweed, are also a welcome addition to the everyday fare. Suitable vegetables for pigeons are lettuce, endive and chicory. A little bit more work, but surely just as good are freshly sprouted weeds. In order to get these, sprinkle some weed seed in a bowl of compost, put it away while warm and damp and wait until the sprouting seeds are a full centimeter above the ground. Put this bowl in the pigeon loft. Not only the young greens, but also some of the compost will be eaten. The latter you will mainly see when the pigeons don't have the opportunity to fly out

freely. In this way you kill two birds with one stone (no pun intended): the pigeons take in fresh vitamins, spore elements and minerals.

Water

Besides food, water is an important element for the pigeons. Right after they have eaten, they will go over to the water container and drink heavily. This is necessary to soften the food in the crop. Therefore you must constantly make sure that fresh clean water is always available in the pigeon loft when the pigeons are being fed. This prevents contamination through polluted water and contributes to the pigeons being in good shape. Don't just get rid of the old water, but also clean the water container thoroughly. Once a week do this a little bit more extensively by using a little chlorine. It is not necessary to add anything to the water but it is possible. Many enthusiasts have good experience with adding a little vinegar or a small drop of chlorine. This contributes to the battle against sprouting germs and viruses. However don't overdo it. If you use chlorine use

The king is able to provide himself with the necessary veggies on the grass

regular chlorine and not concentrated bleach. Also don't add more than 2 cc to a liter (¹/₂ ounce to a pint). If you use vinegar, you should preferably use apple or cider vinegar. This is on the market in various flavors for pigeons. Don't mix it with the drinking water every day, but at most three times a week.

This water container isn't suitable for pigeons

5 PREVENTING ILLNESSES

To prevent is better than to cure

There is a lot of literature about the various illnesses and how they are treated. Most enthusiasts however don't intend on getting well acquainted with pigeon diseases; they would rather prevent them. Prevention is therefore more important than recognizing and being able to treat illnesses. The next section therefore focuses on a number of rules which are necessary to keep your pigeons healthy.

A well cleaned pigeon loft prevents many problems

The pigeon loft needs to be clean and dry

In damp and wet pigeon lofts fungi and bacteria can find excellent nourishment. If in addition to this the pigeon house isn't

Having such dirty nests is asking for trouble

kept clean properly and has manure accumulating then this is asking for trouble. You especially run this risk when you are using a dovecote or a wall-mounted nest box. The physical condition of the pigeons in housing like this will be average to bad and there is increased danger that the pigeons will eat food polluted with droppings. Viruses and bacteria have free reign in an environment like this. The pigeons themselves aren't well feathered in these circumstances and are not very active. The manure we find under the perches is often thin and liquid.

A good atmosphere in the loft

When you enter a pigeon loft you actually shouldn't be able to smell that it houses pigeons. Besides a dry loft, good circulation is very important to achieve this. Fresh air has to be able to flow through the loft – a ventilating grate alone is insufficient. A pigeon loft with an open front prevents this problem. If the front of your loft is closed then you have to make sure that fresh air can flow into the front of the loft at a height of about 40 centimeters (16 inches) and that the polluted air can leave the pigeon loft again via the roof. By applying a construction like this, natural airflow is created and the pigeon loft stays fresh as long as the loft is dry and is being kept clean properly. A stuffy atmosphere in the loft as a result of a lack of fresh air, too many pigeons and pollution by manure cre-

ates an ideal breeding ground for fungi and bacteria. Breathing problems for both the pigeons and their caretaker can be the result of this. The visible result for the pigeons is tightness of the chest.

Nice to look at, but the atmosphere in a dovecote like this is far from ideal

Don't keep too many pigeons

Too many pigeons in a loft results in fights over nest boxes or perches. This creates stress with the result that the physical condition of the animals deteriorates. At the same time the logical result of the overcrowding of pigeons is a higher degree of pollution of the pigeon loft. All this taken into consideration makes for an increased risk that the animals will get sick. There is really only one good solution for this problem: find a new owner for the pigeons of which you have too many as fast as possible. Even better is to never let it reach that point. When you're building your loft you should already have determined how many pigeons you want to keep at most. This number depends on the pigeon loft, how temperamental the breed you want to keep is, the size of the breed you choose and the kind of loft (an opening for free flight or not). The rule of thumb is one cubic meter of loft volume for every pair of pigeons. So when you are building your pigeon loft you already know how many pigeons you can keep at the most. Therefore don't mount any more perches than this previously determined number of pigeons. This way you have an effective means of protecting yourself against a surplus of pigeons in the loft.

The eye of the pigeon tells you a lot about its health

Purchasing new pigeons: Be careful

When purchasing new pigeons there is always the risk of

transference of a viral infection from one pigeon loft to another. Therefore be careful and pay close attention to where the new animals come from. If the animals come from an enthusiast who has his things set up right and you picked them up yourself and ensured that they have had excellent care then you're not going in for a whole lot of risk. If you however buy the pigeons on the market then you have no idea about how the last owner took care of them and you run an added risk because a salesman will have the animals of several enthusiasts together in one cage. To prevent infection of new animals it is therefore prudent to first house the acquisitions separately for a couple of weeks and to pay close attention to the health of the animals. An investigation of the animals' droppings by the veterinarian costs you a little extra money but does exclude a lot of risk.

A healthy pigeon shows well-formed quills

Isolate sick and suspicious animals
If you have a pigeon who reacts sluggishly when you enter the loft, isn't well feathered and stays cowering in its resting place then you should watch it closely. In the morning, check the previous night's production of manure. If it is

Be alert when the pigeon starts to drag its wings

wet, of an unusual color and the pigeon still looks out of shape, then you should take measures. Separate the pigeon and prevent manure from sickbay getting in contact with the healthy pigeons.

Bathe your pigeons regularly

Once or twice a week your pigeons like to have a bath in a couple of centimeters of water. Especially when the weather is nice it is wonderful to see the animals splashing about in the water. Afterwards they lie with their wings spread in the sun to dry. Pigeons can live without bathing but if their feathers are to stay in optimal condition, which is necessary to protect them against all weather influences, then regular clean bath water is not something you should deny them. Add a little bit of bathing salt for pigeons to the bath water and you also achieve an effective means against lice.

A weekly bath bring the quills of the young pigeons into the right condition for flying

6 ILLNESSES, VERMIN AND PARASITES

Illnesses

Despite all your excellent care, it can still happen that the pigeons get sick. Contact with birds, with other pigeons while flying free or transmission of viruses through the air can result in unexpected illness for your pigeons. In general it is true of poultry, to which pigeons also belong, that if an animal is quite ill it has only a narrow chance of survival. As soon as intake of water and food stops the condition, due to the animals' fast metabolism, rapidly deteriorates. Thankfully, the most common diseases are quite recognizable and can often be combated. If your animal is sick and you are doubtful about which illness you are faced with, be smart and contact a vet. Now, not every veterinarian is equally experienced in treating pigeons. There are however, a number of clinics that specialize in pigeon care. These can often advise you by phone after you send them a sample of the pigeon's droppings. So don't hesitate to call on the services of these specialists.

Be wary of pigeons that don't seem to be doing well compared to the other pigeons

All pigeons carry coccidia

Coccidiosis

Coccidiosis is a parasitic affliction which is especially common with poultry, but which can affect all domesticated farm animals. Actually, all pigeons carry coccidia with them. These one-celled parasites burrow into the wall of the intestine. The damage which they do to the cell structure results in a deterioration of the intake of nutrients. If there is a high degree of infection this results in strongly emaciated animals and watery droppings. Along with the dropping, the animals also excrete the so-called "oocysts." Under the influence of heat and moisture these eggs mature very fast. Consequently they are ingested again by the pigeons and the circle is complete. The problem is that these oocysts are difficult to combat. Therefore, every loft is infected up to a degree. Once more, prevention is the best remedy. Prevent food from being infected by the manure through good hygiene. Also don't feed more than the pigeons can consume in half an hour. Always put the food in containers and never scatter it loose on the floor. If you suspect your pigeons might have developed Coccidiosis then you should give them a drinking water cure which you can get from your veterinarian or food supplier. Contamination is easy to determine through an examination of the droppings.

E.Coli-infections

Infections with the E.coli bacteria show themselves through serious diarrhea. The color of this liquidly feces is green. The pigeons become emaciated and sit cowering with their feathers up. The problem is often determining which E.coli bacteria are the culprits. Some strands of E.coli bacteria hardly cause any problems while others can paint a rather serious clinical picture. Some pigeons can become so sick that it results in death.

The infection can be caused by the intake of polluted water or food. This risk is the highest with pigeons that fly free and if you house them in a pigeon loft it is recommended to only let them out if it is almost time to feed them. Most of the time they will quickly return to the loft when you start rattling the food container, which prevents them from

Water from polluted gutters can create an E.coli infection

Pigeon canker can mean the death of your young pigeons – treat the breeding couples preventively

pecking at food and drinking water from gutters and puddles. However, if pigeons are housed on a dovecote this is impossible, therefore you do run a greater risk. Once the pigeons get sick they need a cure of antibiotics as soon as possible, therefore you have to check the droppings daily. If they are thin and green, immediately contact a veterinarian and ask for antibiotics.

Pigeon canker

Pigeon canker is a typical pigeon disease that, in its most serious form reveals itself as a yellow, cheesy discharge in the throat and the corners of the beak. The infection can become so bad that the throat is almost completely blocked. The liver is also seriously affected by the bacteria that cause this disease. The official name is Trichomonas gallinea. With pigeon keepers it's better known as yellow canker. In Great Britain this disease is called pigeon canker, a clear indication of the character of this infection. The infection of adult animals happens through the drinking water. Young pigeons are infected by their parents while feeding. Regularly refreshing the drinking water and thorough cleaning of the water containers is therefore a necessity. A pigeon that has eaten well will always conclude its meal with a visit to the water container. Therefore make sure that every time you feed, the water container is cleaned and filled with fresh water.

This disease can be well and easily prevented. Preventative drinking water cures are for sale in pet specialty shops. If the affliction however is visible in the pigeon loft, then you should be prudent and ask the veterinarian for medication.

Paramyxo

Paramyxo is a serious disease that affects the nervous system. The clinical picture is so severe that keepers of Racing Pigeons are obligated to preventively inoculate their birds if they want to take part in competitions. For Fancy Pigeon keepers there is no such obligation, but it is prudent to make use of the possibility of inoculation anyway. If you ever get to experience the disease in your loft yourself you are sure to resort to inoculation. What is remarkable about this disease is that the animals start to drink a lot. The paramyxo virus also affects the kidneys. The result of the kidney problems and the excessive drinking is a very thin almost water-like discharge. When the disease develops, further paralysis of the wings and feet ensue. The pigeons

Free flying pigeons have a higher risk of being infected by paramyxo

will have a shaking head, keeping it tilted and will have problems with orientation which result in them having problems eating. Recovering from this disease is possible, but often takes a long time and isn't complete. Regular inoculations to prevent the disease are therefore the best method. For Fancy Pigeon enthusiasts who take their animals to compete in competitions, we advise having a veteri-

Where there is food, there are mice – don't leave anything out in the open

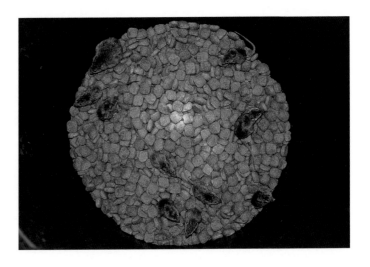

narian give them their inoculations about four weeks before the first inspection. Pigeons are then protected against paramyxo during the whole competition season.

Rats and mice

Naturally, you must keep the pigeon loft free of mice and rats. As early as in the building of the loft and in the materials you choose, try to make it hard for vermin to enter the pigeon loft. However, you also need to make sure it isn't tempting for these animals to visit your loft, simply because there is nothing for them to get. You achieve this by feeding only as much as the pigeons can eat in half an hour; the pigeons are satisfied, they have eaten everything they need and they didn't just go for the most tasty seeds. They leave behind an empty food container that doesn't hold any attraction for the mice and rats.

Slender pigeon louse

The slender pigeon louse is regularly found in pigeons especially at the bottom of the wings and the head. The louse is several centimeters long and quite visible to the naked eye. The lice feed on parts of the feather and can cause holes in them. The slender pigeon louse can be combated simply with a spray or a powder. These remedies can be purchased at a pet specialty store. Repeat the treatment after a week to make sure all lice and their eggs have been killed. Pick up your animals regularly and inspect them for lice. This way you can nip the problem in the bud and prevent the lice from truly becoming a plague.

Small pigeon louse

The small pigeon louse is mainly found around the opening of the anus. If there are many, then they will form a crust by piling eggs. The pigeons become very agitated, peck constantly between the feathers around the anus and are in worsened physical condition. The first sign is roughness of the plumage around the anus; something you will definitely notice if you check regularly. In this case, the lice can also be combated effectively with the sprays and powders that are available in stores. A good way to prevent the small pigeon louse is by supplying bathwater which contains some bathing salts for pigeons.

By taking a bath in sand, the wild Stock Pigeon exterminates lice in a natural way

Bloodmite

The misconception about the bloodmite is that it is not an actual louse, but a mite. You will rarely find bloodmites on pigeons and even then only at night. These mites hide during the daytime in all the nooks and crannies that a loft has to offer. In warm dry weather, the multiplication rate is very high. The mite feeds on blood which it ingests via the skin of the pigeon. If a pigeon loft is heavily infected with bloodmite then a lot of blood will be extracted from the pigeons and their physical condition will deteriorate. For young pigeons this can be so severe that they die. Therefore, check your pigeon loft and the perches regularly for the presence of bloodmite. If you encounter the bloodmites or a grayish residue (the eggs) then you need to take measures. There are a number of sprays for sale which can be used effectively. Make sure to read the instructions properly beforehand, because it may be that you need to keep the pigeons outside the loft for several hours after you spray and that the loft itself needs to be aired properly. Another remedy often applied by many breeders is burning out the seams and other small openings in the loft. Bloodmites and their eggs can't withstand temperatures of more than 60°C. Be careful if you use a gas torch since most

You should regularly inspect the perches and sticks for the presence of bloodmites

A grated floor in
the flight prevents
infections

lofts are built from flammable materials. You should be
aware of the problem of bloodmite when you build your
loft. Seal off all seams so that bloodmite will be unable to
find shelter there.

Worms

In the bowels of pigeons you can also find many parasites.
Roundworms and hairworms can be a problem. If the
worms are to be found en masse, then problems with the
absorption of nutrients will occur. The worms can truly
create a blocking of the bowels. Besides this, they excrete
chemical substances that stimulate the bowels, which have
the negative side effect that the food doesn't stay in the
intestine long enough to be absorbed. Worms lay large
amounts of eggs that ripen outside the pigeon's body in a
warm and moist environment. When pecking at the bottom
of the loft or the flight, the pigeons will be infected with
these ripe eggs and everything comes full circle. If there is a
large chance of infection you will see your pigeons losing
weight. To prevent this infection it is important to keep the
floors of both the loft and the flight from being soiled with

manure. In the loft you can achieve this by cleaning a lot or by applying grated floors. For the flight, grated floors are often the only preventative measure you can take. If you have a sandy floor in the flight then you should have the pigeons dewormed twice a year. The best times to do this are the so-called "dangerous" periods of the year: the warm and wet spring months and late summer.

7 BREEDING

The right season

Keeping pigeons without breeding them is only possible if you house the cocks and the hens separately and don't allow them free flight. For pigeons, the urge to breed is so strong that it impossible to stop them if you house them together. As a matter of fact, being an enthusiast, you shouldn't want to. It is, after all one of the best aspects of the pigeon's social life. You do have to regulate the urge to procreate somewhat, because otherwise too much is demanded of the adult pigeons and the young are born at the most inopportune times. A young pigeon needs sufficient daylight and a temperature that is not too low in order to grow up fast. This means that the months from March through June are the best months to breed pigeons. Earlier or later is possible, but does create a number of problems. Too many young pigeons have died on cold nights against which they weren't yet resistant. By now there are many helpful devices that help to prevent death due to cold nights. There are, for example heated nest bowls, heat mats for inside the nest

March through July is the ideal time for breeding

boxes and of course, heating systems for the whole pigeon loft. The question is however: why all this artificial support when breeding a little later in the year goes almost without a hitch? If the breeding starts even later, the young pigeons often don't grow up completely because the days get too short. This automatically means that the food has to be consumed in a smaller number of hours. This can be adjusted artificially by lengthening the days with lamp-light, but it raises the question of why we would want to do this. Late breeding has a further big disadvantage in that the older pigeons start their moulting too late and they aren't fully feathered by the time the cold wet period starts. It is best just to start breeding in March and to finish at the end of June. This enables you to breed about three nests of young per couple of pigeons. If the breeding goes well, this would mean about five young per couple.

Preparation

A good preparation for the breeding season is the separate housing of the hens and the cocks during the fall and the winter. This means that the loft has to consist of at least two sections. This separation ensures peace and quiet in the pigeon loft and makes the hens stop laying eggs – an ener-gy draining activity. You put both genders back together at the beginning of March. Then the so-called "coupling" begins. The simplest method is bringing together in one space an equal number of hens and cocks and has them pick their partners themselves. The advantage of this system is

Free choice of partners can lead to undesirable color combinations

that the animals don't give any problems accepting each other as partners. The disadvantage is that you have no control and the free choice of partners might result in a serious case of inbreeding, for example brother and sister. Furthermore, random combinations can ensue if you have several breeds and/or colors. A better method is therefore to deliberately put birds together to create breeding couples.

Breeding couples

When creating breeding couples you need to take into account family ties, color and breed. Because you place animals together that might not have chosen each other, they first need to get used to one another before they accept each other as mates. In order to achieve this, the nest boxes need to be designed correctly. Every future couple has to have a nest box available for themselves which can be closed and locked. The size of the nest boxes depends on the breed. There has to be at least enough space for two nest bowls, food and water containers and some scurrying young pigeons. These nest boxes can be placed in several layers on top of each other. The front of the nest boxes should have doors so you can close them and it should be possible to divide the nest box itself into two sections, preferably with a partition made from chicken wire or one with bars.

Breeding in practice

The first thing you do is take all the cocks to the loft into which you placed the nest boxes. Let the cocks choose their favorite nest box themselves. This will take a couple of days and result in a number of fights. The end result will be that the most dominant cocks will occupy the best nest boxes. Usually these are the ones closer to the roof. The advantage of this method is that you don't force the pigeons to occupy a nest box they don't like and that the breeding season proceeds peacefully. Pigeons have good memories; you will notice that those cocks which have bred in these nest boxes before will know exactly which nest box was theirs and they will occupy it again if they get the chance. If you have more nest boxes than cocks you should lock up the remaining nest boxes as soon as the cocks have made their choice. After a couple of days you can add the ladies to the company. In order to force the cocks to agree with your choice, you divide the nest boxes into two parts. This temporary partition should preferably be made from bars. This enables the pigeons to have physical contact, albeit limited. Cock and hen are put into the nest boxes divided by the bars. You lock the nest box itself so the pigeons are forced to stay in each others' company. Most times this results in their accepting each other pretty quickly. After a forced stay of twenty-four hours, you open the nest boxes in the morning and you let your new formed couples loose in the pigeon loft. In the evening you lock the couples in their nest boxes again only this time without the partition. Usually this won't cause any problems and the cock and hen will have found each other. If you notice the hen beating the pushy cock off you should

This pair has found each other

put the partition back. Repeat the process of setting the couples loose in the daytime and locking them back in the nest boxes at night until you notice that all the couples have accepted each other and fly in and out of their nest box independently. For some breeds it is advisable not to work with a series of nesting boxes in a large pigeon loft, but with separate large breeding lofts in which an individual nest box has been placed. Some breeds are so feisty and jealous by character that they will constantly chase the other couples and won't give them any peace. Interruption of the mating will be the result of this which can be seen in the number of unfertilized eggs.

Nesting

Place a nest bowl in the nest box. These you can find in every well stocked pet specialty store. You will also notice that the cocks sit down in this bowl pretty early and start to call their hen. If, besides this you also make nesting material available in the pigeon loft, you will soon be able to see whether or not the pigeons have started to use their nest box. Everything that can be used as building material for a

A Danish
Tumbler in its
nest bowl

nest will be dragged into the nest and consequently shaped into a rather messy nest in the nest bowl. Generally, dried stalks from the tobacco plant are used as the basic nesting material. This material has the advantage that it is not attractive to lice and bloodmites.

Also, small short twigs and similar material are popular with pigeons. It is not necessary to provide nesting material, but it is more natural. Wrapping the nest bowl in a firm layer of paper or placing a special mat in the nest bowl without any further nesting material being available certainly won't keep the pigeons from breeding. Do make sure a clear indentation is present in the nest, because otherwise the

Without nesting
material but
wrapped in
newspaper is also
possible

A pigeon usually produces a brood with two eggs

eggs can easily roll out from under the pigeons while they are sitting on the eggs. There are breeders who instead of (earthen) bowls use wooden nesting crates either with or without a bowl shaped hollow or a bowl shaped inside made of plaster. The advantage of these crates is that you can adapt them to the size of the pigeon breed you plan to breed with. The disadvantage is that mites and lice find a great home here in the seams of these crates. Regular disinfecting is therefore necessary.

Eggs

The first egg often follows soon after the pigeons have been put in couples. The first egg is laid as a rule ten days after the coupling. Usually the second egg follows two days after the first egg. A hen usually lays two eggs. It can also happen that she lays just one egg. If this happens in several nests in a row with the same hen then this is often a sign of decreasing vitality. Heavily bred breeds with a high degree of inbreeding often show examples of this problem. The first egg is guarded well by both partners but isn't sat on yet but rather stood over by both pigeons. Only after the second egg has been laid do they start to sit on them. This way a large difference in age between the first and the second young is prevented.

Two hens might form a couple and give you an unexpectedly large brood

More than two eggs?

If there are more than two eggs in a nest then you have a couple which consists of two hens. Some hens are so dominant that they are accidentally taken for cocks and accepted by the other hen as a partner. They however both start to lay eggs and in that way betray that they have made a fool of you. Even the most experienced breeder has this happen to him. Naturally, the eggs won't be fertilized and you need to go out and find two cocks and couple the pigeons to a male partner.

Check-ups

Both the cock and the hen sit on the egg. The hen does the heavy lifting and sits upon the egg herself the majority of the time. She sits on the nest from evening till morning.

If one egg has not been fertilized then you should let it be until the young is a couple of days old

During the day the cock sits on the egg. Once the eggs have been sat on for about ten days, the time has come to see if there is any life in the egg. This can be easily determined. Carefully lift the pigeon off the nest, but take care not to damage the eggs. A pigeon which is brooding might defend her nest vigorously by beating hard with her wings and pecking determinedly. If the pigeon accidentally hits the eggs with her wings broken eggs will be the result. Therefore you need to use two hands and hold on to the pigeon firmly and lift it from the nest. After ten days of the pigeon sitting on it, the egg should be non-transparent and therefore showing no clear white while lying in the nest. Eggs that still show clear white in the nest bowl and are held in front of a lamp will let light through uninhibitedly. This egg contains no life; it has not been fertilized. A fertilized egg doesn't let any light through and therefore shows a dark mass. With some experience you will be able to spot this on the tenth day when you lift up the pigeon and look into the nest. But don't take any unnecessary risks and stay away from the eggs if at all possible. You can also check if the eggs are fertile at an earlier date. In this case you can shine a light through the egg with a bright light which is called candling. A fertilized egg shows a clearly visible germ and a net of blood vessels already on the fifth day. This candling takes some practice, but when you compare the result of your observation with a non-fertilized egg you will spot the difference pretty fast. If one of the eggs isn't fertilized, leave the brood alone until the young has hatched. If both eggs are unfertilized, then you should remove the brood. After about ten days the hen will start laying eggs again.

They grow fast

Hatching

If everything goes well both eggs should hatch on day seventeen shortly after one another and you will have two young which as yet in no way resemble a pigeon. The first week both parents feed the young with an excretion from the crop, the so-called pigeon milk. The young happen to thrive on this and it is surprising to see how speedily the growth process takes place. Most of the time there is some difference in size between the young. This is related to the different times of hatching, but also with gender; young hens are usually a bit smaller and more delicately built than their brothers. It is often indicated that a couple of young consist of brother and sister. This is generally true when you look at large populations, but nests of young of the same gender do definitely exist. After a little more than a week the parents switch to feeding grain. This is once more fed from the crop. By and by stubble becomes visible on the young pigeons and they become somewhat able to keep themselves warm. In the daytime, the parents stay away from the nest; only at night are the young still covered. This last part can sometimes go wrong because father pigeon is eager to get started on the next brood and starts to pay court

to his lady with a lot of ardor. If it is early in the year and the nights are very cold then it can happen that you will find the young numb with cold or even dead. Therefore, check the nests in the evening and take action if necessary. Closing the nest box with the hen inside and the cock outside is a good remedy.

Just hatched young pigeon; will it have a brother or a sister?

Second brood

Depending on the breed it is possible for the hen to start laying eggs again while the young are still lying in the nest. A second brood while the first brood are only fourteen days old is quite normal with breeds of high vitality. These eggs are simply laid between the growing young if there are no alternatives available. It is better to offer a second nest bowl for this second brood. The hen will be happy to make use of it. This way the eggs stay clean and there is peace in the nest box. Once this second brood arrives you have two choices; letting it hatch or taking it away. Many enthusiasts choose to take the eggs away in order to give their pigeons some rest. If you don't do too many rounds of breeding (the maximum is four rounds per year) then it is quite possible to simply let the pigeons sit on this second brood. A good breeding couple will raise the young from both broods.

Young growing up

Soon the young pigeons will be completely feathered but on all sides the nest down is still sticking out. They will leave the nest and start to roam around the nest box. Make sure food and drink containers are present in the nest box. The sooner they learn to recognize these, the better. The pecking movements of the parents will soon be imitated. If you have nest boxes that are completely open at the front then you will soon find the young pigeons on the floor of the pigeon loft. If the front of the nest box is closed off and they have to leave it over a small plank then this will take a bit longer, but break free they will. You can also decide to take those young that already walk around in the nest box constantly out yourself and put them on the floor of the pigeon loft. They still aren't able to fly at this point, but they can walk. With most breeds it is no problem to have young which are still dependent on the parents roaming freely across the floor of the loft. Only the occasional breed is so fierce that they will attack the young. For these breeds it is

Wild pigeons like this Woodpigeon will never breed on the ground because of the danger

better if they are bred in couples in large breeding cages and to bring the young straight away to a separate loft with only young pigeons as soon as they can eat by themselves. Fortunately, with most breeds this isn't necessary. What you do need to make sure of is that no couples start nesting on the floor of the loft. Some breeds seek out the floor for nesting despite nest boxes being available. As far as the nesting itself is concerned there are no problems, but by putting their nest on the floor they start considering this part of the loft as their territory; they will defend it fiercely. If young pigeons from other couples are walking around the loft and if they come within this "territory" of the floor nesting couple, then they will be attacked and this might end badly.

The nest down still sticks out between the feathers of the young pigeon

*At this age I'm
still ugly, but I
will be beautiful!*

Learning period

The young who have flown out of the nest – or more precisely fallen out – are fed by the parents. Parents and young recognize each other through color and sound. When feeding the older pigeons, the young will walk around the parents and beg for food. The parents will be less and less willing to feed the young depending on the young's state of development. After a while you will notice that they are eating from the food containers themselves. The young are now independent and won't stay on the floor any longer, but hang out at higher locations. Flying is still uncertain in the beginning. However, this improves quickly. At this age they gather many impressions which are of great importance later. If you plan to let the pigeons fly free you should make

*Young German
Long Face
Tumbler in the
aviary*

There has to be enough room for the next generation

use of this learning period and while the weather is good, place the young animals in a so-called sputnik on the outside of the loft. They will then be able to survey the surroundings. After a couple of days you can open the sputnik and let the young out. They can barely fly at this time so there isn't much risk of losing young pigeons.

Departure

If all goes well you have gained a number of healthy young pigeons. Make sure you don't have too many young and that you hand over some to other enthusiasts in time. The problem when selecting young pigeons for new enthusiasts is that you often don't know what the gender of the young is. The only way to get to know this is to wait and see. After a while the young cocks will start chasing the ladies and they start showing they are men by cooing loudly and spinning in circles. However, it can take some time before they display this behavior, which doesn't make the selection any easier.

If the breeding goes well then you will soon have too many pigeons

8 FANCY PIGEON
BREEDS

A large species

Fancy Pigeon breeds come in all shapes and colors. It is a species that worldwide, contains an enormous variation in breeds. An estimate of the number of breeds in Europe alone soon brings us to four hundred. However, worldwide the number of documented breeds probably is closer to a thousand, divided into several breed groups. These have traditionally been chosen based on a distinctive basic characteristic that the breed has in common. If you want to know more or if you are looking for a specific breed then you can get more information and help through the references to internet sites and Fancy Pigeon publications included in this book.

A breed with an obvious balloon is the Norwich Cropper

Cropper and Pouter Pigeon breeds

As indicated by the name, the defining characteristic of all the breeds in this group is the presence of an auspicious crop. Naturally, all Fancy Pigeons have a crop, but usually it isn't or is just barely visible. The breeds in this group however, show their crops very clearly; it is often significantly bigger than in non-cropper breeds. Sometimes they are even so big that we speak of a hanging crop. Most breeds however have a more compact crop which can be filled with air and then swells like a balloon. A group characteristic of all the croppers is that they are very fierce among themselves; show an attractive mating ritual both in the air as in the loft and have a strong connection with their caretaker. The animals are trusting and affectionate, but demand housing in pairs in the breeding season. Well known breeds from this group include the Voorburg Shield Cropper, the Gaditano Pouter, the Marchenero Pouter, the Brunner Cropper and the Reversewing Pouter.

Show Racer breeds

These pigeons have a remarkable body shape as a common characteristic. Many of these breeds have been derived from Homing Pigeons. This means that they were originally animals that were good flyers and that have the instinct to find the way back to their loft over greater distances. The last is however, not as far developed as with Homing Pigeons which have been trained to fly distances. Many of these pigeons are rather firmly built and therefore rather quiet by nature. If you treat them well they will certainly start trusting you, sit with you and start eating out of your hand. These breeds are fertile and generally good at raising their young.

Housing them in groups during breeding is usually no problem. Well known breeds from this group include the Carneau, the Strasser, the Lahore, the Coburg Lark and the German and Dutch Show Racing Homers.

Wattled breeds

A breed name that is somewhat strange, which refers to a striking characteristic in the strong growth of the nostrils and the eye sockets into wart-like structures; something which we don't find in other Fancy Pigeons. This striking growth progresses slowly. The difference between young wattled pigeons and other pigeons isn't very apparent in the first year of their lives. Only in later years a very striking

The typical head of an average Nurnberg Swallow

picture starts to develop because of the continued development of these growths. They can at times become so big that the pigeons start to be bothered by them. As far as character is concerned, these pigeons show a lot of similarities to Show Racers. The group isn't that big with such members as the Dragoon, the Valkenet and the Bagadet.

Hen breeds

Because of a striking, rather high carriage of the tail, the somewhat elongated neck and the horizontal posture, a number of pigeon breeds have a superficial resemblance to chickens. Many of these breeds are rather fierce by nature and don't get along well with one another. Plenty of perches as well as space between them are therefore an absolute necessity. For the caretaker, they are quiet breeds which are very trusting and fly very little. Housing in an aviary is a great solution for these breeds. A disadvantage is that they are rather restless during breeding. Many eggs break and the young don't grow up, mainly with the heavier breeds.

There is some resemblance between chickens and Hen Pigeons

Therefore, these you have to house in pairs. Striking breeds from this group are the King Pigeon, the German and English Modena and the Maltese Pigeon.

Structure breeds

A number of pigeon breeds have very rich plumage which furthermore distinguishes itself because of a deviating feather implant. Examples of this are the Fantail, the Frillback Pigeon, the Saint and the Old Dutch Capuchin. The disadvantage of this deviant feather implant is that it impairs the flying ability of the pigeon. Therefore, we often see Fantails walking on the ground; if you house them on a dovecote, this will mean great losses to cats and predatory birds. It is therefore better to keep them in an aviary. If these pigeons are to show their beauty and grace then you need to put great care into their accommodation. Good perches which prevent the feathers from being damaged are the minimum requirement. These breeds often give a lot of problems with breeding.

The Old Dutch Capuchin is a well-known structure pigeon

Trumpeter breeds

The breeds in this group aren't very striking at first. They don't rely on their good looks, but on the sound they produce. They don't coo, but produce a repetitive sound with a deep resonance that is somewhat reminiscent of a drum roll. Breeds like the Altenburger Trumpeter and the Arabian Trumpeter are very easy birds to accommodate and breed. The Bokhara Trumpeter, which has abundant plumage which makes it hard for it to see and fly, is almost a complete opposite. A nice breed with which people still fly a lot is the Kumru, which originates from Turkey.

Frilled breeds (in Dutch: Gull Pigeons)

The origin of this (Dutch) group name is not altogether clear. Many of the breeds in this group have white bodies and colored wing shields; features that make them somewhat resem-

The front view of the Double-Crested Trumpeter

ble a number of gull species. What all the breeds in this group have in common is the deviating feather structure on the chest. From this, a feather rosette grows in the middle of the chest; a row of feathers going against the grain. This is how the so-called "breast frill" is created. Other striking features of this group are the deviating head shape and the short to very short beak. The latter makes a number of nice, trusting breeds from this group hard to breed. They can raise young that have a normal length beak, but not their own young. Vice versa, their young can be raised by breeds with normal beaks. Fortunately, this doesn't apply to all pigeon breeds. Figuritas, Italian Owl, Old Dutch Turbit and Antwerp Smerle are usually very easy to breed. Oriental Owls however, demand special food and foster parents for their young.

The Thuringer Wing Pigeon is a fine color breed

Color Pigeons

The Color Pigeon breeds are mainly bred based on color and markings. Usually these breeds show many similarities in type. Yet there are large differences among them. There are for example, Color Pigeons with and without feathered feet and Color Pigeons with and without a hood structure on their heads. This hood is formed by a row of feathers that grows against the grain and therefore stands upright. It is unfortunate that many breeds in this group are rather shy.

A rare Chinese Beak-Crested

A red Amsterdam Beard Tumbler

However, this is compensated by the fact that they are great flyers, very fertile and easy to breed. Accommodating them as a group during the breeding season is usually no problem. Well known breeds from this group are the Finch Pigeon, the Ice Pigeon, Saxon Shield Pigeon, Nurnberg Swallow, and the Danish Suabian.

Tumblers and Highflyers

In this group we find breeds that were originally kept because of their striking flying styles. This flying style is hereditary and varies from breed to breed. To be able to really enjoy this group of pigeons you have to let them fly free. Only then will you find out what tumbling, rolling and ringbeating, for example, really entail. Therefore, these are breeds for those who really love flying. The group is rather large and encompasses birds like the Belgian Tumbler, the Danzig Highflier, the Mookee, the Dutch Helmet Pigeon, the Nun pigeon, the Flying Tippler, the Oriental Roller Pigeon, and the Stargarder. If you want to purchase pigeons from this group for flying, then you should make sure to buy them from an enthusiast that selectively breeds on flying qualities. Pigeons from exhibition lines have often been crossbred with different breeds and show their flying style in a diminished way.

9 FLYING WITH FANCY PIGEONS

Flying with Fancy Pigeons

It is often unjustly assumed that Fancy Pigeons are just pretty and that Homing Pigeons are all good flyers. After all, many Fancy Pigeons have a history that is rooted in flying. The flying style of the animals however deviates a lot from that of the Homing Pigeon. Racing Homers are trained to travel distances in as short a time as possible, but for Fancy Pigeons the distance which is traveled is not important. What is important for this group of breeds is the way they fly, the altitude at which they fly and the time they stay in the air as a group. Many of the breeds originally kept for flying already indicate their flying style with their breed name and the way they fly. There are for example Highflyers, Rollers, Tipplers and Tumblers. In order to let the different flying styles come out as well as possible, it is sometimes necessary to make some adjustments to your loft. For example the Tippler, which comes from England and is kept for its ability to stay in the air for very long peri-

Flying is the natural ability of a pigeon

This Beauty Homer Pigeon was originally known as a distance flyer

The Rhineland Ringbeater is a nice attractive pigeon

ods, needs a landing platform on top of the roof that can be seen from great altitudes. Only then will the pigeon be able to find its way back to the loft without problems when the twilight sets in. Every country has its own specific flying styles which over time have been adopted by enthusiasts from other countries; this is simply because of the pure joy that can be experienced from a specific way of flying with pigeons. Germany and Belgium for example, and a couple of other countries know flying with Ringbeaters. This is an ability that can be found in a number of breeds like the Speelderke, Belgian Ringbeater, the Anatolian Ringbeater and the Rhineland Ringbeater.

Ringbeaters

Ringbeating is a form of flying which can be practiced in small spaces. In an aviary which is a couple of meters wide and about 2.5 meters high, a hen is released. Then a cock is also placed in the aviary which will, fiery as it is, perform a mating dance at low altitude above the hen which calmly sits down on the ground in the center of the aviary. This flying above and around the hen is called "ringbeating." The number of "rings" the cock "beats" or in other words the number of circles he flies and the quality thereof determine their value in a competition. This sounds simple, but requires a good physical condition and training of both the hen and the cock. If the pigeons are shy then they will certainly not show this behavior when there is an audience around the aviary. Also, pigeons which are too fat will most certainly not be successful.

Tipplers

A completely different kind of flying with pigeons is endurance flying with Tipplers. Tipplers are rather small pigeons from England which can manage to stay at high altitudes for enormous periods of time, provided the weather is good, because of the right training and by making use of thermic winds. The flying is done in kits: a kit consists of three pigeons. Usually three pigeons of different colors are used which makes it easier to identify individuals when they are high up in the air. The pigeons are trained to stay in the air together. Only when the owner gives a signal are the pigeons allowed to land. The owner's signal is the

A white Fantail is often used as a "dropper"

release of a light-colored "dropper," usually a white Fantail. This dropper hardly does any flying and stays seated on the roof of the loft. The Tipplers have been conditioned to expect the appearance of the dropper and know, "When we see him, there is food!" That signal makes them come down again and return to the loft. The urge with this breed of pigeon to stay long in the air is so great that they will even stay in the air in not too dark nightly hours. With the help of strong lights and a large landing platform the enthusiast ensures that the pigeons can land safely even in the dark. In several European countries, but also in other parts of the world, competitions are being flown with Tipplers. These take place in summer, because of the long hours of daylight and the present thermic winds. Most competitions are held on and around the "longest" day. It's all about which kit stays in the air the longest. Once the pigeons land the competition is over. If one of the pigeons in the kit breaks formation then they are disqualified. The world record is a little more than 22 hours of uninterrupted flying with one kit; that means that these are truly top grade performances which can only be achieved with good, optimally taken care of and long trained pigeons. The advantage of this branch of pigeon sport is that it isn't about having many pigeons, but about well trained small kits. So if you don't have much room available then you can participate in this form of flying even if you only have a small loft. Breeds which are used for this kind of flying include among others the Manchester and the Sheffield Tippler.

Flying with Cropper breeds

Yet another form of flying has been developed with the Cropper breeds. Spanish breeds especially are naturally very fierce in their mating rituals and the cocks have a strong urge to conquer a hen. This characteristic has been used to develop a game that is based on "conquering" the pigeons of a fellow enthusiast. Especially in the west of the Netherlands this form of keeping pigeons has developed itself into a separate branch of the hobby. The whole setup of the pigeon loft is adjusted to this catching of "foreign" pigeons. The cocks are put in small dark boxes and all housed separately. This has the advantage that their natural urges will be at their highest when they come out into the light and see the hen. The hens are kept in somewhat larger boxes with plenty of daylight. The basic loft is rather small and in fact only just big enough for the enthusiast to stand in it and accommodate his hens there. Connected to the loft there is a rather low flight which has been constructed with sliding lids. From the inside these lids are operated with ropes and pulleys. As soon as the hen lands on the flight the lid is closed. The whole construction is mounted preferably as high as possible. In the Hague there used to be many of these lofts high on rooftops. Because of changing building regulations and decreasing interest in this form of pigeon flying, there are only a small amount of these lofts to be found. The game which is being played with the pigeons basically comes down to when a "foreign" pigeon is in the air you have to recognize what it is. If it is a hen, then you release your own cock which will start to pay

The dark boxes for the cocks which are housed in the flight

The Gaditano is an example of a Spanish Cropper breed with good flying abilities

court to the hen, loudly flapping its wings. The Spanish Cropper breeds are so fierce that they don't give up their mating dance quickly. If the cock is successful in luring the hen to his loft and if both of them land in the flight then the game is over and the prize has been won. The captured pigeons are sold to a local merchant after which time the original owner has the opportunity to buy his own pigeon back. This mating dance in the air is a magnificent sight which appeals to many enthusiasts. Sometimes the appeal is so strong that they also build similar installations in different countries. It first becomes really attractive when there are several enthusiasts within flying distance. The pigeons which are traditionally used are crossbreeds. Nowadays, pure, recently imported breeds like the Gaditano, Granadino and the Laudino Copper are being used with increasing frequency.

Highflyers and Tumblers

This catching of other peoples pigeons' is also a game with a long history in Amsterdam. However, they don't fly with Cropper breeds, but with Highflyers and Tumblers. Here too they put the catching contraption as high as possible on the roof, preferably on the cam. The catching of the pigeons isn't done in a flight, but in a so-called "purse." This "purse" is perched on top of a small box. In this box the enthusiast can't do much more than stand. This so-called "closet" has glass walls so the enthusiast has an unobstructed view in all four directions. The flat roof of the "closet" with the purse on top forms a suitable landing platform for the pigeons. The "purse" consists of an ingeniously hinged latticework and is somewhat comparable to the closing mechanism of an old-fashioned wallet. From the inside out the purse is opened and closed with the help of strings. Breeds like the Dutch Highflier, the Amsterdam Tumbler and the Hague Highflier fly from this purse. The object of the game is to send a couple of your own birds into a flock of unknown birds in the expectation that your couple will bring back home a number of the "foreign" pigeons which, after they have landed on the flat roof, are caught in the purse. This form of flying is also becoming rare because of changing building regulations and because the design of houses in the larger cities has been altered. Yet despite the restrictions there is more and more interest in flying with pigeons. This increasing interest has caused a fun development: flying with pigeons on a so-called "flightbox."

Flightbox

The origin of this branch of the pastime lies with the army. In the beginning of the twentieth century, they made use of transportable boxes with Carrier Pigeons; this in order to

Pigeons on the purse

*The Amsterdam
Closet with the
purse on top*

enable communication with the home base from the field. The (Carrier) pigeons that were housed in these boxes were trained in flying from different locations and always returned faithfully to the transportable box. This fidelity to its "own" box isn't dependent on the dimensions of the box, which means that a small, easily transportable cage can also meet the requirements. Therefore, they could make use of pigeon baskets which were taken into the field on the back of a courier. This is the idea behind the flightbox. Even before the pigeons are able to fly they get used to the flightbox in which they find food and water. Feeding is only done on and in the flightbox. The box itself is painted a bright color so it is easy to recognize out in the open field. The team of pigeons that fly on the box is supplemented with a striking white or colorful pigeon that hardly flies itself. Usually this is a Fantail or a Fantail crossbreed. When this pigeon, the so-called "dropper" is put on top of the box, this signifies for the flying pigeons to come in and eat. With the box and a well trained team you can fly in practically any location. There are international competitions where the enthusiasts fly with their boxes and their teams of pigeons to places agreed upon. A good breed for flying on the box is the Oriental Roller, but also many Tumbler breeds can be gotten used to the flightbox. If you don't have the opportunity to offer your pigeons free flight at home then this is a possible solution. You will certainly have a lot of spectators when you let your pigeons fly on a nice summer day in the city park only to let them return on command to your flightbox an hour later.

The team of pigeons that fly on the box is supplemented with a striking pigeon that hardly flies itself

The pigeons are fed on or in the flightbox

Young German Show Racer Pigeons of about a week old

10 CLUBS

Why a club?

As an enthusiast you are always looking for the reasons behind some of your pigeon experiences. On the internet and in books you can gather a lot of wisdom. However, translating this theoretical wisdom to your own pigeon loft isn't always as easy. A desire to exchange experiences with seasoned breeders and to learn from them often soon asserts itself. These contacts can be established in many different ways. The easiest method by far is to get in touch with an association of small animal keepers or a specific pigeon keeping association.

The local association and national specialty clubs

Fancy Pigeon enthusiasts are often affiliated with a local association that also accepts breeders of other animal species. Through these associations they procure their rings. These rings enable them to give each animal its own unique distinguishing mark, which for example makes it possible to register them in a breeding account. The local association often makes sure there is the possibility of having the pigeons collectively inoculated against one or more diseases. The connected costs are lower because of the collective activity than when you have to have the inoculation performed privately by your own veterinarian. It is of

The Voorburg Shield Cropper has breed associations in many different countries

course possible that this local association has few Fancy Pigeon enthusiasts as members. The specific knowledge about the breed you are keeping and breeding is then often not available. This knowledge is then more easily acquired through a national breeding association or a specialty club. These are clubs in which enthusiasts of a breed or of several breeds which belong to the same group come together.

Where to look?
The national association of small animals or more specifically, pigeon enthusiasts, has internet sites in most countries with links to local associations and breed associations.

Exhibitions

It is also possible to establish contacts with Fancy Pigeon enthusiasts by visiting exhibitions. In the fall and winter months, exhibitions are organized all over Europe. This can be a small local exhibition with only a few hundred animals, but also a very large one that is specifically dedicated to Fancy Pigeons. Here you often find many thousands of Fancy Pigeons and there is a large chance that the breed that you are interested in will also be present. Between the cages it is easy to find fellow enthusiasts with a preference for "your" particular breed. Specifically visiting these large exhibitions has various advantages. First of all, you find a large collection of Fancy Pigeons which will have expertly written comments on the attributes of their breed. This commentary has been administered by a well trained judge and enables you to acquire good insights into the differences between a high and low quality pigeon. The larger shows also have a special sales category or otherwise some of the exhibited animals will be for sale. Exhibitions therefore offer you a chance to purchase a number of new animals. You can also find various salesmen who sell everything you need. Pigeon lofts, material for the interior of the loft and food will often be for sale in the stands of the various companies and this enables you to compare price and quality of the products. The dates, locations and opening times of especially the larger national exhibitions you can find through the internet sites of the national associations or the breed associations. For local exhibitions you need to rely on advertisements in the local newspapers.

11 IMPORTANT ADDRESSES

Fancy Pigeon sites on the internet

* **National Pigeon Association in USA**
  www.npausa.com

* **National Pigeon Association in Great Britain**
  www.zyworld.com/npa

* **Australian National Pigeon Association**
  www.anpa.com.au

* **South African Fancy Pigeons Association**
  www.mjvn.co.za/safpa

Veterinarians specialized in Fancy Pigeons:
David E. Marx D.V.M.
Golden Valley Pet and Pigeon Clinic
2707 NW 60th Ave.
Norman, OK 73072
1-900-737-MARX
USA

Gordon A Chalmers,
DVM
Lethbridge,
Alberta, Canada.
e-mail: gachalm@telusplanet.net

Pascal Lanneau - Veterinarian
Kerkstraat 21 8552 Moen Belgium
Tel: 0032 56 649143
Fax: 0032 56 774577
E-mail: pascallanneau@skynet.be

Magazines
Feathered World
http://www.winckley.co.uk/index.htm
– Internet magazine

Purebread Pigeon
http://www.purebredpigeon.com/
- Internet magazine and also a full color magazine
(published bimonthly, six issues per year)
Purebred Pigeon
PO Box 3077
McKinney, TX 75070 USA

12 CONSULTED SOURCES, ACCOUNT OF PICTURES AND A WORD OF THANKS

Acknowledgements from the author

While writing this I had a lot of help and support from the home front and from many pigeon enthusiasts. A special word of thanks goes out to my wife Ineke for correcting and critically reading my typing and for guarding the "timeline" of this writing job. I also want to thank Esther Verhoef for challenging me to write a second book. Furthermore, my thanks go out to Claudia Pelsmaeker who supported me with an important part of the photography. Of course she wouldn't have been able to take her pictures without the selfless cooperation of a number of excited Fancy Pigeon enthusiasts. Special thanks go to the following breeders: D. Bosman, G. Bosman, H. Klijnsta, E. Krol,

G.A. Krol, H. Meerman, D. Pot, E. Pot, G. Siemons and A. Steenhuis. Furthermore, I want to thank the photographers Renate Hagenouw and Janine Verschure and the breeders that let them take supplementary photo material: Martin van Uden, Ton Heesters, Theo v.d. Boogaart, Rinus Peijs, Rikus Hagenauw, Michel Roggeveld and Tuinland Groningen. Lastly, thanks to all the Fancy Pigeon enthusiasts who, unbeknownst to them, have contributed to the creation of this book. In many discussions about the keeping and caretaking of Fancy Pigeons, they have provided me with material that enabled me to write a well-founded book.

Literature

To create this book the following sources have been consulted: the site of the Dutch Association of Fancy Pigeon Enthusiast clubs (www.sierduif.nl), the site of Racing Pigeon club "De Gouden Leeuw" from Nieuw Vennep (http://pvdegoudenleeuw.tripod.com), the site Oropharma in Maastricht (www.oropharma.com/nl/duiven/html), a site about the Danish Tumbler by Wim Halsema (www.home-pages.hetnet.nl/~wim_halsema), a site about Helmet Pigeons written by Albert Pennings (www.geocities.com/nederlandse_helmduiven), a site about the English Nun Pigeon by Henk van der Vegt (www.geocities.com/nonduif), a site by Fred Zandiga about Portuguese Tumblers and Takla Rollers (http://home.wish.net/~fredzandinga), the site of the Voorburg Shield Cropper Club (www.sierduif.nl/voorburger), Sierduiven, by R.R.P. van der Mark; Sierduiven, by Ben Mulder and Jan de Jong; Prisma Duivenboek by Dr. Thijs Vriends; De 500 mooiste duivenrassen van A tot Z by Hans-Joachim Schille and Josef Wolters; various issues of "Avicultura", the magazine for small animal keepers, publisher Avicultura in Amerongen; various issues of "Fokkersbelangen," the magazine for the small animal enthusiast, a publication of the Dutch Small Animals Publications and the ready knowledge of many excited pigeon enthusiasts

Photographs:
Claudia Dispa: 7-13, 16 below, 19, 20 both, 21 right, 27-30, 35, 36, 40, 41, 43, 45, 46, 49 above, 51-56, 61, 62, 64, 65, 67-69, 72, 73, 77, 78, 80-83, 86, 87, 88 above, 89-92, 93 below, 94 both, 95 both, 97, 98, 103-107, 108 left, 115 above, 116-119, 121, 126.
Renate Hagenouw: 14 left, 21 left, 32-38 above, 48, 79, 112, 124, 127.
Aad Rijs: 6, 14 right, 15, 16 above, 17, 22, 24, 42, 71, 96, 110, 111, 113, 114, 115 below.
Ellen Uittenboogaard: 26.
Esther Verhoef/Furry Tails: 18, 34 below, 39, 49 below, 50, 54 below, 59, 63, 70, 74 both, 76, 84, 85, 88 below, 93 above, 109, 125.
Janine Verschure: 23, 25, 37, 38, 47, 58, 60, 66, 75, 99-102, 108 right, 120, 123, 128.